Our FLAG

By Wendy Svec

MODERN CURRICULUM PRESS
Pearson Learning Group

The following people from Pearson Learning Group have contributed to the development of this product:

Art and Design: Dorothea Fox, Jennifer Ribnicky

Editorial: Leslie Feierstone Barna, Nicole Iorio, Patricia Peters

Inventory: Levon Carter

Marketing: Alison Bruno

Production: Roxanne Knoll

All photography © Pearson Education, Inc. (PEI) unless otherwise specifically noted.

Photographs: Cover: *t* © Dan Thornberg/istock photo, *b* © Blend Images/Punch Stock; 4–5: © Blend Images/Punch Stock; 6: © Granger Collection; 8: © Lee Foster/Alamy; 12–13: © Bettmann/Corbis; 15: © Photo Researchers, Inc. Illustration: 11: Betsy Day.

ISBN-13: 978-1-4284-1296-5

ISBN-10: 1-4284-1296-4

Printed in the United States of America
1 2 3 4 5 6 7 8 9 10 11 10 09 08 07

Modern Curriculum Press
Pearson Learning Group

1-800-321-3106
www.pearsonlearning.com

Contents

What Is a Flag?

It is the morning of the Fourth of July. You go to see a parade. Soon some people in the parade pass by with a **United** States flag. Then the high school band comes by. A young boy holds the flag of the high school. Other people in the Fourth of July parade have flags, too.

Many of the flags in the parade are different from each other. However, the flags are the same in one way. Each of these flags is a **symbol** that stands for another thing. Flags can be a symbol for many different things. Many flags are symbols for a country or state.

People often wave
flags to show their
love for their country.

Flags were first used in **wars**. People in an **army** could look for a flag. They could see where the army for their country was. The army could tell which flag was theirs by the flag's color. A flag could have one or more colors. The army would also look for the **design** on the flag. The design could be a picture or it could have stripes or shapes.

In a war an army often calls its flag its "colors."

Our Flag Today

The **American** flag colors are red, white, and blue. The flag design has 13 long red and white stripes. The stripes are a symbol for the first 13 states in the country. There are 50 white stars in the top left part of the flag. Each star stands for one of the 50 states. That is what the American flag looks like today.

Flag Rules

If the United States flag is on the same pole as a state flag, the United States flag must be on top.

How Our Flag Came to Be

Our country once had several flags. Before we had states, our country had **colonies** that were ruled by another country. Many of the colonies had their own flag. In 1775 the colonies went to war with the country that ruled them.

After the war, the colonies were free. They became states. The United States got a new flag that had 13 stars and 13 stripes. It had one star and one stripe as a symbol of each state.

In 1795 two new states became part of the country. Each state got a star and a stripe on the flag. The flag now had 15 stars and 15 stripes. People in the **government** knew there would be more states. With more states there would soon be too many stripes.

When the United States first became a country, its flag had 13 stars and 13 stripes.

In 1818 the government made a new rule for our red, white, and blue flag. Every new state that became part of the United States would get a star. The stars would be in rows. However, there would always be 13 stripes. These stripes are a symbol of the first 13 states.

Flag Rules

People may hang the American flag with the top side down only when they need to show that they need help.

The United States flag has added a star to its flag each time a new state has become part of the country.

1777
13 STARS
1818
20 STARS
1848
30 STARS
1896
45 STARS
1912
48 STARS
1960
50 STARS

Francis Scott Key felt happy to see the American flag fly after a hard fight in 1814.

More Than a Flag

In 1814 the United States was in another war. One morning after a very hard fight, a man named Francis Scott Key saw an American flag. He was happy to see the flag fly. He knew that the Americans had won the fight.

Francis Scott Key wrote about what he felt when he saw the flag. He called the flag a "star-**spangled banner**." *Banner* is another word for *flag*. His words were made into the song "The Star-Spangled Banner."

Like the flag, "The Star-Spangled Banner" is a symbol of our country. People sing it at many different places and times. People sing it before ball games. People also sing "The Star-Spangled Banner" on important days such as the Fourth of July.

The red, white, and blue American flag is a symbol for the United States. It can mean many things to the American people. To some Americans it means the right to be free.

Americans use the flag to show their pride in the United States. You see the star-spangled banner at schools and places of government. People hang it on ships and on homes. To fly the flag is to show your pride in our country.

Flag Rules

In 1949 the government named June 14 as Flag Day.

Even young Americans can help fly flags.

Glossary

American having to do with America

army people who fight in wars

banner a flag

colonies places where Americans first lived

design the way that something is made

government people who run a state or country

spangled with light or a shine

symbol something that stands for another thing

united made into one

wars when armies from two or more sides or countries try to win